THE
Archive Photographs
SERIES

PICCADILLY
CIRCUS

"EROS", PICCADILLY CIRCUS, LONDON.   19374

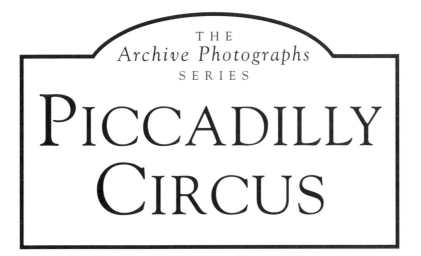

THE
Archive Photographs
SERIES

PICCADILLY CIRCUS

Compiled by
David Oxford

For Joan with love

CHALFORD

First published 1995
Copyright © David Oxford, 1995

The Chalford Publishing Company
St Mary's Mill, Chalford,
Stroud, Gloucestershire, GL6 8NX

ISBN 0 7524 0196 3

Typesetting and origination by
The Chalford Publishing Company
Printed in Great Britain by
Redwood Books, Trowbridge

Acknowledgements

Thanks are due to the following for permission to reproduce the pictures on the pages listed (L = lower, U = upper):

British Pathe News, 58L; Joe Cornish, photographer, 94L; Richard Delahoy, photographer, 90L; E T W Dennis & Sons Ltd., 81L; FISA(GB) Ltd., 88L and 91; Guildhall Library, Corporation of London, 8U; Hallmark Cards Ltd., 86L; Kardorama, 83, 84U, 85L, 86U, 87, 89, 90U, 92L, 93, 95L and 96L; J Salmon Ltd., 82L; Selfridges Ltd., 41, 54 and 57U; Thomas Benacci Ltd., 92U, 94U, 95U and 96U; Raphael Tuck and Sons, 10L, 12L, 23U and 69; Walter Scott (Bradford) Ltd., frontispiece and 65U; Whiteway Publications Ltd., 94L.

Much of the history of Piccadilly Circus described here was drawn from *A History of Regent Street*, by Hermione Hobhouse (Macdonald and Jane's, Queen Anne Press, London, 1975), to whom many thanks for her permission and also for her encouragement and advice.

Other sources:

David Kaye, *Buses and Trolleybuses before 1919*. (Blandford Press, 1972)
John Reed, *London Buses Past and Present*. (Capital Transport, Harrow Weald, 1988)
Who's Who in the Theatre. (Pitman, 1912 to the present)
Leslie Halliwell, *Halliwell's Film Guide*. (Harper Collins, 1977 onwards)
Survey of London. (Athlone Press)

Contents

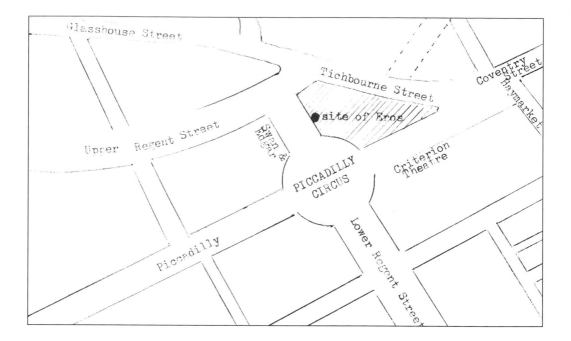

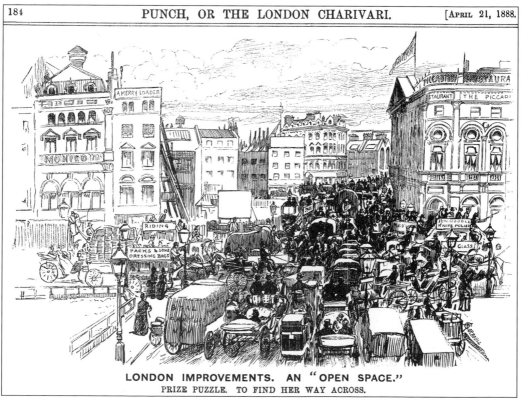

LONDON IMPROVEMENTS. AN "OPEN SPACE."
PRIZE PUZZLE. TO FIND HER WAY ACROSS.

Introduction

For the past 100 years, Piccadilly Circus has provided one of the most popular postcard views for London's visitors to send home with their hurried greetings. The famous Eros statue was unveiled in 1893, shortly before the introduction of picture postcards in 1894. In those early days, when London was the capital city of the British Empire, Piccadilly Circus was often described as "the centre of the world". It used to be said that if you stood there long enough you would see everyone you knew.

Originally a small circular road junction, the Circus was expanded to its present size and shape in the 1880s. Quite remarkable changes were made to the street-plan of London; a whole block of buildings (the shaded area, opposite), forming one quadrant of the original Piccadilly Circus, was demolished, and a new thoroughfare – Shaftesbury Avenue (indicated by the broken lines) – was driven north-eastwards through Soho towards Bloomsbury.

In the new "circus", which was now three or four times its original size, and no longer circular, Sir Alfred Gilbert's aluminium statue of Eros, the god of love, was set on a fountain pedestal as a memorial to Lord Shaftesbury. The old London Pavilion, pulled down to make way for Shaftesbury Avenue, was replaced by a new London Pavilion on the triangular site next to Shaftesbury Avenue.

The *Punch* cartoon of 1888 (opposite), which shows a view across the Circus and along Shaftesbury Avenue, with work still in progress, suggests some contemporary public reaction to the "London improvements". The Monico Restaurant, on the left, has displayed the familiar Coca Cola sign since about 1955, and the Amery & Loader building (labelled by the cartoonist, with the heavy humour of the late nineteenth century, "A Merry Loader"), was later hidden behind the Guinness clock from 1932 to 1972. Compare this with the upper picture on page 86, which is from the same viewpoint.

The effects of the demolition are shown clearly overleaf in two views of the Circus taken before and after the work was carried out. The upper picture, one of the few illustrations in the book which is not a postcard, is an archive photograph from the Guildhall Library. The lower picture taken in 1886 would not have been published as a postcard until about 1894.

This is the view along Coventry Street from Piccadilly Circus, about 1880. Originally Regent Circus, it had by this time already been named Piccadilly Circus, as a name-plate below one of the upper windows shows. On the right is the Criterion Theatre, and in the left half of the picture is the block that was soon to be demolished.

An early postcard shows the same view in 1886, after the demolition. With the removal of the north-east quadrant of the Circus, the site beyond it, with the new London Pavilion, can now be seen. At this time, the Shaftesbury Memorial Fountain (Eros) had not yet been installed.

One

Early Days

London – Piccadilly Circus

A Gardening and Forestry Exhibition at Earls Court, advertised on the nearer bus, dates this view to the summer of 1893; the other bus bears a sign indicating its route as Baker Street and Piccadilly, and the fare: one penny. Eros is surrounded by a low wall bearing a commemorative plaque for the Earl of Shaftesbury (1801-1885). As Anthony Ashley Cooper, he was a Member of Parliament until he succeeded to the title in 1851, and his life was largely devoted to improving the lives of working people, particularly through the reform of working conditions in factories and the establishment of workmen's institutes and schools for the poor.

This is mid-1895, and the omnibus on the right advertises *The Girl I Left Behind Me* at the Adelphi. The low wall around Eros was removed earlier in the year, and the flower-sellers are already well established. The aluminium statue, which was silver in colour in 1893 (see page 9), is beginning to darken after two years of London smog.

The Circus looks spacious when seen from the Coventry Street end, with the London Pavilion on the right and the Swan and Edgar building straight ahead. As the correspondent writes, "Don't this look a fine place...." On early postcards like this one (the view is *c*. 1896), the back of the card was for the address only, and any message had to be written on the front.

There are some thirty horse-drawn vehicles in this photograph, taken in 1897 – and how many in the whole of London? And how many street-sweepers to keep the roads clean? The London Pavilion now advertises Spaten Beer from Germany; a telegraph messenger drinks from one of the water fountains which spout continuously from around the plinth of Eros, using one of the chained cups provided.

LONDON—PICCADILLY CIRCUS.

In 1899, a newsboy's placard announces the "Latest from Windsor" – probably the racing results – and a "Greater Britain" exhibition at Earls Court is advertised on the omnibus. The upper basin of the fountain, which was full in 1897 (see page 11), is now empty. The upper-level fountains were little used after this period because, on windy days, the water would spray the passers-by, and the flower-girls had to use umbrellas.

PICCADILLY CIRCUS.

You could cycle safely across in those days. You could also run across in front of a bus, like the lad on the left, if you were prepared to be sworn at by the driver.

A playbill for *The Wild Rabbit* at the Criterion dates this view 1899. A white noticeboard above the doorway of the building beyond the Criterion announces that it is to be the site of an Underground station entrance.

Piccadilly Circus.　　　*E.D-L*

The pavement and steps around the fountain were usually crowded – one could buy flowers, drink from the fountain, catch a bus, or just sit.

14

In front of the flower-sellers, a shoe-black kneels, awaiting customers. Van Raalte at number 2, where a window-cleaner is working, is a hat shop. Everyone wore a hat in those days.

From an upstairs window of Swan & Edgar, we look down the length of Lower Regent Street to Waterloo Place. Across the road, the Great Northern Railway office advertises tickets for all parts of Scotland and the North of England and for MacBraynes steamers for all parts of the Continent, while next-door the South Western offers admission tickets for the Crystal Palace, and passage to Paris for the Paris Exhibition. The sandwich-board man on the pavement outside is advertising premises to let.

Two

The Edwardian Scene

Piccadilly Circus.

One of a series of stereoscopic views, this card shows Piccadilly Circus in 1901.

26 LONDRES — Picadilly circus

This is a rare French postcard showing a busy scene in 1902. It illustrates the skill and authority needed by a point-duty policeman in the days before traffic-lights. If necessary, of course, he could speak to the drivers, who were all in the open air. An omnibus near the fountain is advertising *The Little French Milliner* at the Avenue Theatre.

The bootblack has a customer (look between Eros and the hansom cab).

The Criterion Restaurant and the Criterion Theatre on the south side added to the attractions of the Circus.

The Wrench Series No. 2258. Photo W. P. Dando.

London   Newspaper Boys waiting for th

Every newspaper-boy in the West End appears to have joined this gathering to await the first

pecial Edition", Piccadilly Circus

issue of the *Football Echo*.

PICCADILLY CIRCUS.

MARIE TEMPEST.

Ogden's *Guinea Gold Cigarettes*.

In 1903, Marie Tempest was appearing in *Caste* at the Criterion Theatre. Born in 1864, she became a distinguished singer in light opera; at the turn of the century she turned to comedy, and continued as a successful actress into the late 1930s. She became Dame Marie Tempest DBE in 1937, and died in 1942. The cigarette card (left) was issued in 1899 or 1900.

LONDON. PICCADILLY CIRCUS.

With a 1903 view, this card is possibly the earliest to show a motor-car in the Circus, although by this time they were a fairly common sight; one or two heads are turning, but it does not appear to cause any great sensation.

A view (about 1904) from the front of the London Pavilion shows the new theatre front added about 1900.

Taken in 1904, this photograph shows clearly the sets used for paving the road surface. They appear to be the same stone sets that were visible in 1880 (see page 8). Motor vehicles were uncommon at this time, but the Circus was by no means quiet – the noise made by iron-clad wheels and hooves on this surface can be imagined.

The same view a minute or two later. The man who was standing near the lamppost, wearing a boater and carrying a paper, has stepped a little closer to the camera, and the policeman has emerged from the crowd to appear in the foreground of the photograph. He is definitely not smiling, however, possibly because he is worried about the obstruction of the traffic emerging from Piccadilly, since the photographer's tripod must be in the middle of the road.

In the background is a 'bus with an advertisement for a display of Brock's fireworks at the Crystal Palace. This is therefore probably a day in late summer, and two ladies and a girl in white dresses and white hats appear to be enjoying the bright sunshine, while many of the men are wearing straw boaters. The young man on the tricycle-cart, left of centre, only *appears* to be cycling backwards – he is actually going forwards.

A Sports Exhibition at the Crystal Palace dates this scene to 1904. There is by now a black

PICCADILLY CIRCUS

noticeboard announcing the proposed site for the Underground station, just beyond the Criterion, replacing the white board which we saw in 1899.

This is a horse-bus of Thomas Tilling, Job-Master*, of Peckham, about 1905. The diamond-shaped advertisement on the rear of the bus is for Carter's Little Liver Pills ('worth a guinea a box').

* Job-master: one who keeps a livery stable, and hires out horses and carriages.

This postcard appears to be an amateur production, because the picture is askew and off-centre. The photograph, however, has a professional appearance, possibly because the camera was held not much more than half a metre off the ground.

A Thomas Tilling motor-bus, on its way to Peckham, passes through Piccadilly Circus. Tilling's Peckham and Oxford Street route was the first to be wholly motorised.

110   LONDON. — *Piccadilly Circus.* — LL.

On the Love Path, advertised on the 'bus, is playing at the Haymarket Theatre in September 1905. A lad with a tricycle-cart, between the 'bus and the camera has dismounted and is standing with hands in pockets, in the middle of the road. The publisher has given the postcard below, which is different, the same serial number.

110   LONDON. — *Piccadilly Circus.* — LL.

The same view a little later. Now that a cart has moved out of the picture, we can see that on the left there is a Carter Paterson horse-drawn van also standing stationary in the road, with reins hanging loose and no sign of the driver. The lad is apparently watching his horse for him while he is away. It is interesting to conjecture the reason, particularly as there is now another Carter Paterson van visible to the right of Eros.

Types of London Life (4). Flower Seller at Piccadilly Circus.

Why did the flower-sellers use these long sticks? To reach the upper decks of the omnibuses, where the gentlemen mostly rode (no smoking inside). Presumably the flower-ladies caught the money in their hats.

This is 1906, and at last the necessary demolition has been carried out and the Underground station entrance built. There is a 'To be let' sign on top of the entrance, which must obviously refer to the space above.

In the same year *The Dairymaids* opened at the Apollo Theatre. It is advertised on the Union Jack 'bus on the right which is just entering Shaftesbury Avenue, and which will pass the Apollo probably within less than a minute.

This was photographed from an upper-storey window of the Monico restaurant, looking down on half-a-dozen hansom cabs, a four-wheeler, and a motor-car.

AT PICCADILLY CIRCUS. *7 October. 06.*

A Darracq Serpollet steam omnibus enters Upper Regent Street. Metropolitan ran many of

these steamers during the years 1907 to 1911, but this is an early Pioneer which was running in 1906. It burned paraffin, and had to be started by heating with a blow-lamp on cold mornings.

PICCADILLY CIRCUS, LONDON.

The scene is 1908. The motorbus to the left of Eros is advertising a revival of *The Dairymaids*, this time at the Queen's Theatre. The cyclist who is holding on to the rear of the bus for a free pull up Shaftesbury Avenue is almost invisible in a dense white cloud of exhaust fumes

10514—11   PICCADILLY CIRCUS, LONDON.   ROTARY PHOTO. E.C

The definition in the original of this remarkable 1909 photograph shows not only every detail of the lettering on the London & North Western Railway goods and parcels collecting van in the lower right-hand corner, but also (with the aid of a hand-lens) the advertisement for *Fires of Fate* at the Apollo, carried by the horse-bus which is just entering Shaftesbury Avenue, and the title of the play above the theatre itself, which is distantly visible about 100 yards along Shaftesbury Avenue (see enlargement, right).

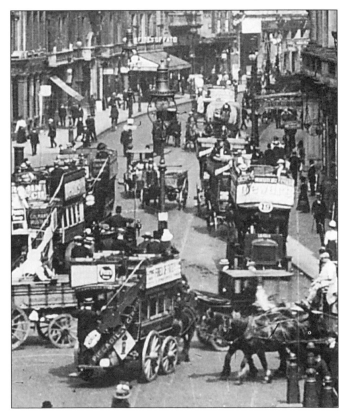

The cash registers offered by NCR in the advertisement on the 'bus, with prices starting at £4, look like a bargain; they would be prized antiques today. On the other hand, the four gold sovereigns necessary to buy one would now be worth about two hundred pounds.

This is another 1909 view. Swan & Edgar's stands like a castle in the background. In the foreground, the tyre-tracks reveal how dirty the road surface is; the street-cleaner with a spade does his best until the quiet of night-time allows the water-carts to wash it down.

Three

1910 to 1914

2486. *Piccadilly Circus, London.*

This is 1910, and motor-buses outnumber horse-buses for the first-time; of London's 2,300 buses, 1,200 are motorised. As early as 1893, the Monico Restaurant and other premises carried illuminated advertising signs, but now we see this form of advertising used for products not connected with the businesses concerned. The authorities frowned, but the leases had been drawn up before such use of electricity could be imagined.

It is still 1910, and the summer sales are on. The two buses in the foreground, advertising a "stocktaking sale" at Hamptons the drapers, are a Vanguard and a Union Jack, while the bus beyond Eros, advertising King C Gillette's new safety razor, is a General. The competition among numerous motorbus companies would continue until 1929, when the London General Omnibus Company was to take over the last of its rivals. This postcard was posted in 1918, long after it was first published.

The postmark is 14 November 1918, three days after the armistice, and the message reads: "Well, my old Celestin, that's it for this time. Here's our old France delivered from all the Boche soldiery and one can breathe now and think about a new era. What do you say about it? No more war! A hearty handshake to my old mate, and remember me to Mother and Father Debelle. Your friend, Amedee".

Piccadilly Circus, London.

This is Wednesday, 13 July 1910, and an *Evening News* placard, held by the man standing in front of Eros, reports "Airship Disaster, 5 Killed". That day, the airship Erbsloeh exploded near Leichlingen in Westphalia, killing its owner and crew of four. Prior to working on the problems of airship navigation, Herr Erbsloeh was a well-known balloonist, and won the Gordon-Bennett race from St Louis across the Rocky Mountains in 1906.

By coincidence, another aviator who had competed in the 1906 balloon race was killed on the previous day, Tuesday 12 July 1910, while flying the Wright biplane in which he had recently made the first ever Dover–Calais–Dover flight. He was Charles Stewart Rolls, joint managing director of Rolls Royce Ltd. From that time onwards the well-known RR logo above the Rolls Royce radiator was coloured black instead of red.

A 1911 scene shows one of the last surviving horse-buses. It ran from Charing Cross to

Waterloo Station and the Elephant and Castle. Note the babe-in-arms, dressed in white, on the upper deck.

King George V acceded to the throne in 1910 and was crowned in 1911. The bus in the foreground advertises the Coronation Exhibition at the Great White City, Shepherd's Bush. The Underground station has by this time been finished with a projecting roof over the pavement, and the upper storeys have been rebuilt.

Swan & Edgar's, "the leading West End drapers", were decorated with flags and garlands and specially embroidered "G.R." drapes for the Coronation. A fine carriage with liveried and top-hatted coachman stands waiting for its owner to emerge from the shop.

In September 1911, Master Noel Coward, at the age of 10 (going on 11), was appearing in *The Great Name* at the Prince of Wales Theatre; the bus on the right carries an advertisement for the play.

On a foggy day, probably in the winter of 1911/12, a father and daughter pose for the camera.

Piccadilly Circus, London

It is 26 April 1912, two weeks after the loss of the *Titanic*; the newspaper-boy's placard tells of the latest development in the strike aboard her sister-ship, the *Olympic*, whose crew are concerned about safety and the provision of lifeboats.

The placard reads: "*Olympic* saloon passengers going ashore – 12 o'clock edition". The ship being strike-bound in the docks, it was decided to take the saloon passengers off, and accommodate them ashore.

46

Piccadilly Circus, London.

It is 1913, and judging by the number of straw boaters being worn, this is a fine summer's day. The time by Saqui & Lawrence's clock is seven minutes to four.

Piccadilly Circus, London

This picture is apparently by the same photographer; the clock says five to four, the same group of people appear on the steps to the right of Eros (one, a lady in a long white skirt), and the camera angle is the same (note the street lamp in the foreground, right). The photographer sold each view to a different publisher – this was a common practice, judging from the number of such 'pairs' that exist.

A policeman holds up three identical taxicabs in a near-perfect straight line.

This privately produced postcard shows two smart young men, who appear to be brothers, posing by Eros in the summer of 1913. James Welch is the star of *Oh! I Say!* at the Criterion Theatre – the show is advertised on a flower-seller's sunshade.

10508—53   PICCADILLY CIRCUS FROM REGENT STREET,   ROTARY PHOTO. E.C.
SHOWING CRITERION RESTAURANT, LONDON.

Looking from Upper Regent Street we see a great variety of vehicles. Several taxis have the white-walled tyres which became fashionable about 1911 and were to remain in vogue well into the 1930s.

Photographed in 1913, this is one of the earliest genuine night scenes. Many publishers had previously created 'night-time' views by darkening daylight pictures and adding lamplight effects. Frank's, the barbers, who first leased the upstairs premises from about 1911, were a well-known feature of the Circus for thirty years or more.

These buses are passing in front of Swan & Edgar in May 1914; one advertises the "Sunny Spain" exhibition at Earls Court. Many of London's double-deckers would soon be taken to France for use as military transport, these possibly among them.

BUSY PICCADILLY, LONDON.   No. 9.

Here is a very crowded scene shortly before the outbreak of war in 1914.

648.Y. PICCADILLY CIRCUS, LONDON.
SITUATED AT THE JUNCTION OF REGENT STREET AND PICCADILLY, THE CIRCUS IS IN THE MIDST OF THE WEST END
THEATRES AND PLACES OF ENTERTAINMENT.   ABOVE ARE SHOWN THE FAMOUS "CRITERION" RESTAURANT AND THEATRE,
LONDON PAVILION, AND IN THE DISTANCE LEICESTER SQUARE.   THE SHAFTESBURY MEMORIAL FOUNTAIN IS A
TRIBUTE TO THE GREAT PHILANTHROPIST

At first sight this is the same view as above, but none of the 'buses in the upper picture appears here. However, the distinctive white van parked in front of the London Pavilion strongly suggests that it is the same day. No clock is visible, but a signboard above the circular window on the corner acts as a sundial and shows that this was the later picture by about five minutes. The flower-sellers' white sunshades carry an advertisement for the 'New Gallery Kinema'.

Still in 1914, we look down from the top of the Criterion building at a very orderly traffic flow, even though the only policemen visible are both giving directions to enquiring pedestrians.

Four
Between the Wars

PICCADILLY CIRCUS, LONDON.

No new views of Piccadilly Circus were produced in the years 1915-1917. This is 1918 or 1919; *As You Were* is playing at the London Pavilion, and *Tails Up* at the Comedy Theatre is advertised on the bus in the foreground. The war appears to be all but over, and there are many British and French military uniforms among the crowds.

28872   **PICCADILLY CIRCUS, LONDON**

This is another beautifully clear photograph, taken on a sunny afternoon in 1919. Its definition is so perfect that on the original card one can read (with a lens) the title of Ian Hay's play, *Tilly of Bloomsbury*, above the Apollo Theatre in Shaftesbury Avenue, and also *The Voice from the Minaret*, which is playing at the Globe Theatre, the farthest building visible.

In 1920 a bus carries an advertisement for John Galsworthy's *The Skin Game* at the St Martin's Theatre. At the top of the Monico building is an advertisement for *The Times' The Women's Supplement* – women had won the right to vote as recently as 1918. Outside Swan & Edgar's a Chelsea Pensioner, who may possibly have served in the Crimean War of 1854-1856, passes two sandwich-board men who had very probably served in the first World War.

**Shaftesbury Memorial Fountain,
Piccadilly Circus, London**

169

Photographed in late June or early July 1921, this postcard gives a fine view of the detail in the fountain pedestal, and also a review of 1921 fashions.

56

Piccadilly Circus at Night, London.

By 1922, the illuminated signs are numerous: Bovril, Schweppes, Old Orkney Whisky, Muratti's cigarettes, Sandeman's port, Glaxo baby food, Pirelli tyres, Paripan paint, Venus pencils, *The Evening News*, 'Snake Charmer' cigarettes, and an Overland motor car (priced at £220), all appear in lights in this photograph, as well as the signs for Saqui & Lawrence, the jewellers, and the Monico Restaurant.

In 1923, there are fresh advertisements for Hennessey's Brandy, New Pin soap, and Pinnace cigarettes, with a Bonzo Dog logo. It is noticeable that this type of advertising was confined to the north-east side of the Circus; the leases of the buildings on the west and south, which are on Crown land, did not permit it. *The Times*, in 1928, described the lights as "a hideous eyesore which no civilised community ought to tolerate .....", but the popularity of the "Piccadilly lights" perhaps explains why most photographs of Piccadilly Circus are taken from the south or the south-west.

LONDON.– PICCADILLY CIRCUS.

The film showing at the London Pavilion in 1924 is *Wanderer of the Wasteland*, filmed "entirely in Nature's colour". The 'bus advertises the appearance of Ivor Novello, the Welsh matinée idol, playwright and composer, at the Prince of Wales Theatre. He was born Ivor Davies, in 1893, and died in 1951. He composed the music for *Glamorous Night*, wrote and composed *Careless Rapture*, and, surprisingly, wrote dialogue for the film *Tarzan of the Apes*.

London - REMOVAL OF FAMOUS STATUE "EROS" FROM PICCADILLY. *1164*

Later in 1924, Eros was removed to the Victoria Embankment Gardens, to make way for large-scale development of Piccadilly Circus. The flower-girls, too, were obliged to leave; a few remained around the outside of the Circus, some moved to Leicester Square, and some to a site near Park Lane.

S.15955.   EROS IN THE VICTORIA EMBANKMENT GARDENS, LONDON, W.C.2.

Eros was to remain here from 1924 until 1932. Meanwhile, below the Circus, the new concourse was constructed, including a much enlarged Underground station, while above ground many of the buildings surrounding the Circus were reshaped.

This aerial view before 1924 shows the Circus in its 1890s shape, with the original (circular) Piccadilly Circus still visible, marked by three of the old quadrants.

From the same angle in 1928 the Circus shows considerable change; the Swan & Edgar building has been rebuilt as a rectangular block; the County Fire Office (the building just beyond Swan & Edgar) has been redesigned with three arches in place of the original five arches, and the buildings at the top of Lower Regent Street have been squared off, thus removing the last vestiges of the nineteenth-century Circus. At the same time, extensive alterations have been made to the Regency facade along the whole length of Upper Regent Street.

In 1928, Noel Coward, by now a world-famous playwright, actor, lyricist, composer and director, has *This Year of Grace* at the London Pavilion. Eros is still absent. Below ground, the new concourse is nearing completion, and will be opened in December.

In 1929, *Wake Up and Dream* is playing at the London Pavilion. The matching designs of the new Swan & Edgar building and the County Fire Office can be clearly seen in this view.

Cochran's 1930 Revue is at the London Pavilion. In the lower left of the photograph is a sign with a cross and the words "Cross here" – this was a forerunner of the Belisha Beacon (introduced in 1934, although not in the Circus), and the light-controlled crossings introduced later.

This view is still 1930, but the postcard publisher has removed the date from *Cochran's Revue* (so that his postcards will not look 'dated'). He has also, with considerable skill, prematurely reinstated Eros; even under a strong lens, the illusion is complete, except that the statue appears to be standing in the road, its base hard up against a bus.

Looking into the Circus from Lower Regent Street, we see arrows painted on the road surface to indicate the direction of traffic flow. They are widely used today, but these are some of the earliest, and poorly designed. They appear to indicate that this is a one-way street, with the right-hand side for traffic going ahead only.

This gives a closer view of Shaftesbury Avenue, in the spring of the same year. The film poster advertising William Powell (still remembered for his role as detective Nick Charles in the Thin Man films, with Myrna Loy co-starring as Mrs Charles, and with Asta the dog) in *Street of Chance*, emphasises that it is an "all-talking" film. The first film with a sound-track, *The Jazz Singer*, had been released only three years earlier.

Shaftesbury Avenue, from Piccadilly Circus, London
209368 J.V.

In 1932, the Guinness clock is being installed; the hands and the numbers XII and VI are in place, and the workmen's cradle can be seen on the clock face. Eros had been replaced on a new octagonal base, slightly further east and sixteen inches higher.

The Guinness clock's title, "Guinness Time", above the clock face, has now reached the first 's' of Guinness. The clock will remain there for forty years. Noel Coward's *Cavalcade*, which opened at Drury Lane in the autumn of 1931, is still running, and is advertised on a poster displayed in Shaftesbury Avenue.

An interesting poster on the right-hand side of Coventry Street reads: "Crime and banditry, distress and perplexity, will increase in England until the bishops open Joanna Southcott's box". Joanna Southcott (1750-1814) imagined herself to be the woman referred to in the Book of Revelations, whose son would "rule all nations with a rod of iron". She left a box to be opened in the presence of a number of bishops "during a period of national crisis". The box was opened in 1927, but was said to have contained nothing of significance. However, her believers claimed that it was the wrong box, and the campaign continued into the 1930s.

A policeman holds up the traffic for pedestrians using the crossing in 1933.

In Upper Regent Street the traffic is heavy as it enters or leaves Piccadilly Circus, which is visible in the distance.

To cope with the increasing traffic problems, a "gyratory traffic system" was introduced in the Circus in 1926 and was later (1934) reinforced by "safety lanes" painted on the road surface.

The 1935 film, *Folies Bergere*, with Maurice Chavalier, is showing at the London Pavilion. The postcard's title describes Piccadilly Circus as "the Centre of the World".

The traffic appears to be even heavier in 1937, and requires a constable at each junction – there are seven streets entering the Circus. No fewer than nineteen buses are visible in this photograph, all of them belonging (since 1933) to London Transport: in that year Herbert Morrison's London Passenger Transport Bill set up a Board to take over the London General Omnibus Company's fleet and all Underground services.

Later in 1937 a phased traffic-light system was introduced, and is said to have replaced thirteen constables.

It is still 1937: this card shows the Eros fountain, as well as the Criterion Restaurant and Lillywhites, decorated for the Coronation of King George VI and Queen Elizabeth (now HM Queen Elizabeth the Queen Mother).

PICCADILLY CIRCUS

In the summer of 1939, the film at the London Pavilion is *Elephants Never Forget*, starring Oliver Hardy (without Stan Laurel).

PICCADILLY CIRCUS LOOKING DOWN
SHAFTSBURY AVENUE, LONDON.

248

It is late summer, 1939: the "Huge Success!" advertised by the illuminated sign on the left of this picture refers to the well-known *Illustrated* magazine, which was first published at the beginning of March in that year. Unfortunately, the blackout would soon put the illuminated sign out of action, but *Illustrated* continued successfully during the war, and for thirteen years afterwards.

Five

The Forties

In 1941, we see the fountain (extreme left) boarded up, lamp-standards painted black and white for visibility in the blackout, car headlights hooded, and windows around the Circus showing signs of damage from a bomb which fell in Upper Regent Street in September 1940.

Piccadilly Circus, London

Posters around the memorial fountain, showing the searchlights and shellbursts of an air-raid, urge citizens to "Hit Back!" by buying National War Bonds.

THE HUB OF LONDON, PICCADILLY CIRCUS

"What can I buy? – War Savings, of course!", says one poster, and "Wings for Victory", says the other, picturing Lancasters and a Spitfire. The lamp-standards have no lamps – they were removed for the duration of the war. The heavy globes were taken down because they could not be used under blackout regulations, and they represented a possible additional hazard for the Civil Defence Services (Police, Fire, Rescue, ARP) during air-raids. After the war, the premises at No 44, below the Guinness advertisement, were to be occupied by Boots the Chemists, but in this picture they are holding a "Soviet Youth" exhibition, and there is a portrait of Stalin in the window.

PICCADILLY CIRCUS, GIRLS AND BOYS ON LEAVE

Here are some very welcome visitors, their proudly-worn USAAF uniforms contrasting with the British squaddy's baggy serge.

PICCADILLY CIRCUS, WORK AND PLAY

There is no-one in this picture who is carefree, although some manage to appear so. These were the days of long hours, shortages, air-raids, shipping-losses and bereavement – the "darkest days".

It is 1945: the war is over. Ingrid Bergman appears in *Spellbound* at the London Pavilion, and the still boarded-up fountain advertises for recruits to the Palestine Police at £20 per month.

Eros returned at the end of June 1947 from safe wartime storage in Egham.

In 1948, Eddie Cantor is starring in the film *If You Knew Susie* at the London Pavilion. A poster in Coventry Street announces the appearance of Dinah Shore (1917-1994) at the London Palladium. The tall white posts visible on either side of the entrance to Shaftesbury Avenue are in readiness for pennants that are to be put up to celebrate the Olympic Games, which were held in London that year.

119901.   A GENERAL VIEW OF PICCADILLY CIRCUS AFTER THE "GREAT SWITCH ON".

Illuminated advertisements were blacked out during the war, and were prohibited after the war because of the need for fuel economy. This regulation was ended in the spring of 1949, and on Sunday, 3 April, a delighted crowd gathered to watch the lights of Piccadilly Circus switched on for the first time in nearly 10 years.

PICCADILLY CIRCUS, LONDON. BY NIGHT.

One hour later, and the crowds are still there. They have good reason to celebrate, as this event symbolised the beginning of the removal of wartime restrictions – clothes rationing had just ended, but canned goods, petrol and soap continued to be rationed until 1950, sweets and sugar until 1953, and meat and bacon until 1954.

Six

The Fifties

The Festival of Britain was held on the South Bank from May to September 1951. Throughout that period the Eros fountain was turned on at low pressure so that the water cascaded down its sides.

The time is autumn 1951. The Circus is a popular place to have one's photograph taken, as the young lady is doing – her young man with the camera is behind the girl in the white jacket. They could have saved their film and bought the postcard!

6.   LONDON LIFE: A Flower Seller in Piccadilly Circus.

One of the last of the flower-sellers at Piccadilly Circus, about 1952.

Mr V G S George, possibly the last shoeblack in the Circus, about 1952.

Left: This is an amateur photograph of the illuminations around Eros.

Below, left: In 1953 Eros was decorated and illuminated for the Coronation of Her Majesty Queen Elizabeth II.

Below, right: The Coronation coach passes through Piccadilly Circus.

EROS FLOODLIT, LONDON.   22.14.18

THE CORONATION OF HER MAJESTY QUEEN ELIZABETH II
THE ROYAL COACH ENTERING PICCADILLY CIRCUS

In 1955 the first Coca Cola sign appears, and the Guinness clock has a new design, with two sea-lions juggling the zoo-keeper's pint ("My Goodness!"). The traffic appears to be snarled up.

Half a minute later, and not much has moved.

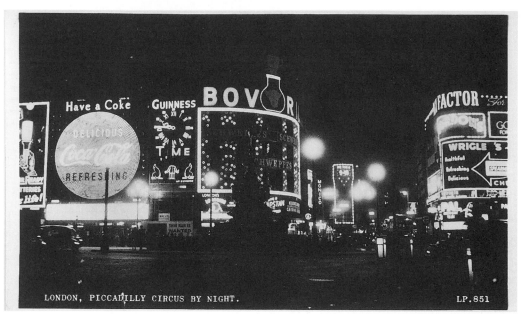

LONDON, PICCADILLY CIRCUS BY NIGHT.   LP.851

The animated Piccadilly lights are frozen in time; but, for the spectators, the Coca Cola sign whirls and flashes, the Guinness sea-lions juggle, the Schweppes bubbles rise, and the Wrigley's arrow moves, while the Gordon's Gin and Lemon Hart Rum signs spell out their messages letter by letter, all in coloured lights, and the Bovril sign alternates between its two trademarks, one of which is the famous Bovril bottle that "prevents that sinking feeling".

PICCADILLY CIRCUS, LONDON

By 1959 the Guinness clock is a Swiss cuckoo clock with a swinging pendulum. *Some Like It Hot* is showing at the London Pavilion.

82

Seven

The Sixties and Seventies

This 1960 view shows the Piccadilly lights reflected in the wet road surface.

In 1961 a new traffic-flow system is introduced, with the fencing-off of a roughly triangular area which includes Eros.

Another view of the fenced-off section in 1962. The compulsory left turn out of Shaftesbury Avenue seems to have eased some of the problems.

By 1963 the new central area is paved. The film *Tom Jones* is showing at the London Pavilion.

It is 15 October 1964 and the election results (courtesy of *The Daily Telegraph*) are flashed up on the front of the Criterion – they show Labour 179, Conservatives 119, Liberals 2. Roughly half of the results are in – can Labour win again at last, after thirteen years out of office? Harold Wilson was summoned to attend on Her Majesty at Buckingham Palace the next day, and shortly afterwards moved into Number 10 Downing Street for the first time.

Piccadilly Circus, London.   Kardorama Ltd.

1965 and the office block Centrepoint rises in the background.

Help! at the London Pavilion (John, Paul, George and Ringo appear to be spelling it out in semaphore signals of their own devising).

1967: with its new enlarged refuge in the middle, the Circus now has pigeons, presumably an overflow from Trafalgar Square.

Piccadilly Circus, London.   Kardorama Ltd.

1968: Centrepoint stands completed, and *Goldfinger* is showing at the London Pavilion. The water was flowing again in the Eros fountain during the late Sixties. Here we can see five ladders leaning against the octagonal pedestal, and there are possibly three more behind it – but no-one seems to be interested in what the invisible owner of the ladders is doing.

PICCADILLY CIRCUS, LONDON

By 1972 the Guinness clock has gone, and there is a new Coca Cola logo. The Wrigley's advertisement has been redesigned twice since 1965.

1973: a buses-only lane across the central reservation has not only eased the traffic-flow, but seems to have got rid of the pigeons too.

We take a last look at Swan & Edgar on the left; the building is soon to be taken over by Tower Records.

In 1975, the premises below the four dark windows on the left of the picture, which were occupied by Boots the Chemists in the early Fifties, and which promoted Air India during the Sixties, are now apparently let out on short leases – the present occupants call their business "Kleptomania". The whole of this frontage will soon be extensively refurbished, the Coca Cola sign will be re-sited to cover the dark windows, and Boots the Chemists will return to their old premises.

Piccadilly Circus, London

Everyone who remembers the summer of 1976 will remember this hot, dry weather. Visible at the far end of Coventry Street, the trees of Leicester Square offer cooling shade.

This privately produced postcard has a good portrait of the familiar Routemaster bus, photographed in 1977.

Eight

Recent Times

1980: the London Pavilion, its upper storeys having been cleared of all advertising in 1977, once more appears as it did in 1893 (see page 9).

About 1982: Tower Records are now established in the Swan & Edgar building.

By the summer of 1986, Piccadilly Circus has had yet another major change. Eros was removed in the autumn of 1984 for urgent repairs and restoration by experts in Edinburgh. Meanwhile, the traffic lanes of the Circus were completely reshaped; then, in March 1986, Eros was restored to his plinth at the new site, some forty feet eastward. No longer isolated, but included in a paved area in front of Lillywhites, he is more accessible to visitors, and is now visible to anyone approaching along Shaftesbury Avenue or along Piccadilly.

Piccadilly Circus
London

About 1986: sunbathing, picnicking, watching the world go by. The Philips advertisement has been removed, to make way for Foster's lager.

Piccadilly Circus
London

The same day: Piccadilly Circus has a flower-girl again – but only for the day.

1987: an unusual angle, showing the entrance to Piccadilly at upper right. Passers-by pause to look at a pavement artist's work.

Here we can see the new road layout and traffic flow, which is northward and eastward only. Traffic approaching along Shaftesbury Avenue is diverted before reaching the Circus.

This illustrates very well how the Eros fountain, is its new position, is now visible the length of Piccadilly, which is the street immediately ahead.

Many things have changed over the years, but not out of all recognition; the Monico Restaurant is now a Burger King, and in the former premises of Saqui & Lawrence, the jewellers, H Samuel are carrying on a similar business.

Piccadilly Circus

LONDON

Piccadilly Circus, at the heart of London's theatreland, is still, after 100 years, a popular meeting-point. It used to be "I'll see you outside Swan & Edgar's"; the new meeting-place appears to be "outside Lillywhites", but be careful where you stand on a windy day, because these days the upper-level fountain jets are running continuously again.

This is Piccadilly Circus as it is today, viewed from the same angle as in the 1888 *Punch* cartoon on page 6. The London Pavilion now houses a museum of popular music, and effigies of pop stars stand on the first-floor balcony. From left to right they are: Michael Jackson, Diana Ross, Buddy Holly, Elton John, and (over the main entrance) Gary Glitter.